Heart of the Prairie

Minot, Jamestown, Valley City and Devils Lake

Volume Three
North Dakota Centennial Series

Published by
**The Dakota Graphic Society
Fargo, North Dakota**

Text: Nancy Edmonds Hanson
Photographs: Sheldon Green
  Russ Hanson
Production: Leonard Roehrich
Historical photographs: State Historical Society of North Dakota.
Printer: Knight Printing Company, Fargo.

Dakota Graphic Society
Box 9199
Fargo, North Dakota 58109
©1985 by Dakota Graphic Society. All rights reserved.
I.S.B.N. 0-911007-07-5

CONTENTS

Introduction . . . . Lean Country

Chapter One . . . . Bones of the Buffalo

Chapter Two . . . . Crossing Over

Chapter Three . . . . Coming Home

Chapter Four . . . . From Fjords and Steppes to the Prairie

Chapter Five . . . . Surge of the Cities

Chapter Six . . . . Dryland Farms and Homegrown Industry

Chapter Seven . . . . Punctuating Nature

LEAN COUNTRY

At the heart of the prairie lies lean, rough land.

Scarcely two hundred years have passed since explorers claimed it as their dominion, sketching its contours on their peculiar maps of the mysterious North American interior.

Indian ponies beat tracks into its toughened turf across the first of those centuries, following a thundering tide of bison. Railroads scored its hide with their long deep tracks, and wagon wheels cut deep ruts. The decades of concrete highways can be counted on the fingers of two hands; air routes and rural telephone wires fit onto a single one.

Always, the prairie has been there mostly to be crossed. Its theme has been vastness; its melody, the toneless rush of rustling grass brightly lit by songbirds; its chorus, the irresistible American urge to press farther west.

Only as the lands on its margin were saturated with settlers and cities would this land, too, be filled up to its brim with the first generation intending to stay. Then, in a steady rhythm of promise and despair, it would spill over. Long slow trickles of lost families would move on.

The North Dakota heartland has felt the bite of a thousand plows and heard the hammers of a hundred hopeful towns. Like its prehistoric seas and the modern floods that punctuate its spring, prosperity has ebbed and flowed with the weather and the tide of human affairs.

The will to tame it has not always been enough. The best-laid plans have sometimes sunk beneath its potholes and its rocks. This central core of the North American prairie has delivered up dry years, and lush, fertile valleys, and hillsides seasoned with stones; century-long family dynasties, and disenchanted dreamers heading deeper toward the west.

And occasionally it has given ground to tough-willed optimists building their villages and their farms, as its grasses inevitably gave way before contagious sweeping fires. Yet even amidst the deep-rooted farms that tenaciously cling along its flanks, it still affirms the dispassionate creed and spirit of prairie ... never entirely broken to harness, never completely tame.

This country is not cozy. It does not comfort. At heart the prairie remains the same perplexing, daunting, challenging, breath-taking landscape that reckless wayfarers once resolved to carve into chunks.

The United States was raw and brash and young then. The prairie was ageless. Even where humans have won with stubborn reason and endurance, the prairie still prevails.

It is a lean rough rolling land of great distance, great challenge and great unblinking sky, and it does not easily yield itself to fragile claims and deeds.

All North Dakota calls itself a prairie, but the claim is truest at its heart.

The broad central swath of counties sweeps from the international border at the 49th parallel to the South Dakota limit, both arbitrarily justified by politics rather than geography. Naturally, though, the region swings much wider. To the right, it marks off the edge of the most northern philosophical outpost of the true Midwest. To the left, it leads toward the undeniable demarcation of the westerner's state of mind, beginning at the Missouri River.

― Heart of the Prairie ―

Caught between this pair of rather different views of the world, the land itself is of two minds. Bits of both Midwest and West surface here. Caught between the flat deep silt of the Red River Valley and high harsher buttes of the Missouri Slope, the central prairie borrows from each but stands distinct from either.

Rich deep-green valleys cut like butter through the rise of semi-arid hills, tracing the course of rivers like the Souris, Sheyenne and James.

Cattle graze among still cornfields where ten million buffalo once made the earth quake. Sunflowers and flax and wheat throw a grid of blue and gold where waving needle-and-thread grass, bluestem and grama once wove their carpet.

Yet the same spunky wild roses and purple coneflowers and black-eyed Susans still bloom in the ditches and poke up through broken piles of granite pushed up by winter's frost. Those rocks, gathered years ago with back-breaking effort, are timeless too — stacked on the margins of fields as silent monuments to pioneer farmers' battles.

The naturally-wooded shores in the Turtle Mountains and along Devils Lake contrast dramatically with their treeless pothole cousins, strewn with marshy abandon across the state's midsection.

The horizon line does vary, despite the claims of those without the time to seek its subtleties. Nearly-level meadows at the state's center are gradually shouldered by a corps of hills and brushy coulees that commemorates the apex of a final glacier's career and the beginning of its end.

Toward the north central region, most farms are manicured and shaded. In shaggy hills toward the south and west, they as frequently testify to the western homesteader's ethic — to make do, to press hard, and to invest more dreams in the land than in the four-walled creature comforts that would merely sit upon it.

———————— Heart of the Prairie ————————

Once the prairie's silence secured its threat to swallow and engulf puny two-legged plowmen and cattle herders. Today, linked to the rest of the nation by automobiles and insurance policies and television, its stillness contains relief.

Yet it covers the same old complex, quiet paradoxes.

Cross-prairie drivers can occupy the hours entranced, staring due north or south or east or west, hands unswerving on the steering wheel, foot heavy on the gas . . . and never glimpse a horizontal curve nor sight another soul. Nothing moves. Yet overhead one of the continent's great parades takes place each autumn and spring, when millions of wings speed feathered travelers along this busiest of migratory bird highways.

Water has frequently been scarce. Yet at sunset the horizon glows red and golden with reflections from uncounted shallow ponds. Seen from above, the land is as freckled with reed-ringed potholes as a leopard is with spots.

Even its rivers are of two minds, at a minimum. The Souris, heir to an ancient lakebed past as dramatic as the Red River Valley's, meanders south and east before scurrying back to its Canadian origins like the foraging mouse for which it was named.

The James and Sheyenne get their start as neighbors in the region of Devils Lake, snaking southward in sinuous step like a sister act. But then they clash over separate suitors along the Height of Land. The James chooses the Missouri, casting its lot with the Mississippi and the Gulf of Mexico. The Sheyenne slides toward the Red, its flow rolling northward into Hudson's Bay.

They comb a part through these dry hills that divides the flow of waters from north to south as immutably as the Rocky Mountains' rift between east and west. Here, though — like the gentle shifting of gears from well-watered farms to all-out arid ranching — the pace endorses the subtlety with which this region changes its mind.

Change is gradual, but absolute, when the calm broad prairie goes about its business.

Des Lacs National Wildlife Refuge, Kenmare

Today, buffalo again roam the heart of the prairie on the Sully's Hill National Game Preserve near Devils Lake. (left)

BONES of the BUFFALO

In the beginning the heart of the prairie belonged not to the Sioux hunters who ranged across it, not to the European monarchs who claimed it, not to the great trading companies that carved their outposts or to the green young American nation far toward the east... but to the buffalo.

Each new frontier has had its destiny set by its geographic blessings. California had its coastline, Montana its mountains, Minnesota its timber, Alaska its gold. In the absence of all of these, Dakota Territory could boast of bison by the millions.

It was a bounty so unexpectedly enormous that it left early witnesses grasping for words to describe its scale.

Trader Alexander Henry told of riding out all day through a crowd of beasts so free of fear that they barely blinked at him, all in an unsuccessful attempt to find the great herd's edge. "At daybreak I was awakened by the bellowing of buffaloes," he wrote in his journal of the year 1800. "The ground was covered at every point of the compass as far as the eye could reach, and every animal was in motion."

The earth shook beneath their feet. Six feet tall, ten feet long and each tipping the scales at a generous ton, the bison was an irresistible force. Herds of tens of thousands surged across a land where no barrier could thwart them.

Nineteenth-century observers estimated that from fifty million buffalo to nearly three times that number roamed the grassy domain from Texas into Saskatchewan and Manitoba. The planet had never seen a species to match these tough-hided, shaggy-haired natives. In its prairie grasses it had produced the perfect menu to nurture them; in their movements it had found a perfect partner to populate its broad slow-featured vistas and muddy watering holes.

In formidable size and sheer numbers the buffalo found a defense against virtually any natural threat. Wolves and mountain lions might pick off elderly or injured animals from the herd's straggling rear guard. Blizzards and other perils of the plains might occasionally thin their numbers, and Indian hunters might target them as prey during long expeditions to stockpile the winter's provisions. But the number lost were miniscule and easily replenished by the next spring's crop of sturdy long-legged calves.

The buffalo ruled over the Dakota prairie for centuries beyond counting. But as the American frontier pushed its way beyond the humid croplands and onto the prairie the stage was set for slaughter on a scale that humanity had never imagined...a mindless wholesale destruction that in a matter of one generation would reduce the buffalo to a nearly-extinct historical curiosity and leave the prairie strangely quiet, strangely steady and inconsolable by its absence.

That humans could destroy so awesome a resource, and so quickly, seems unbelievable today. Yet pressed by Canadian buffalo-hunting caravans of Metis in North Dakota and by hordes of commercial hunters on the southern plains, the herds were depleted far beyond their ability to sustain themselves.

The Sioux had stalked the buffalo to provide all the necessities of their nomadic lives, and it had been an even match. Metis and white riflemen shot them for their choicest flesh, or their hides, or for sport and challenge. Killed by the thousands in a single bloody day's work, the bison's once-awesome natural privilege melted before the forces of gunpowder and gluttony.

What was left was legend...legend and bones. Settlers who arrived on the northern plains in the 1880s and 1890s learned of the millions of brave beasts that had

Early settlers sold tons of buffalo bones to buyers stationed at railroad crossings throughout central North Dakota. These Minot stockpiles were photographed in 1889.

rumbled over the earth they plowed not only in old-timers' stories, but in the fields themselves. Buffalo skeletons lay half-buried in the sod like the silent stones left behind by glaciers.

Gathering those bones — a market-ready "cash crop" — helped sustain the dream for many a hard-pressed prairie farmer in the early statehood era. Ghostly piles greeted travelers at most central North Dakota railroad stations, waiting for shipment back east for use in sugar-refining. A single buyer estimated in 1891 that in the past seven years he'd purchased the skeletons of nearly six million animals.

Today remainders of the great herds, which had teetered on the very brink of extinction a century ago, remain in scattered refuges and zoos here and around the world. Without the last-minute protection of the same species which had pushed it to the edge, the bison would live today only on the American nickel...a fitting tribute, perhaps, to the imperative that erased it from the plains.

The tailrace of Baldhill Dam north of Valley City provides a bountiful brunch of dizzied fish for members of continent's largest nesting colony of pelicans from nearby Long Lake, a wildlife refuge tucked between the valleys of the Sheyenne and James Rivers.

Though the bison are all but gone, the birds are here to stay in all their sky-frothing glory.

The heart of the prairie suits birds as well as buffalo. The same early diarist who marveled at them documented clouds of waterfowl, geese and smaller birds darkening the landscape in colossal migrations each spring and fall.

North Dakota's heartland lies in one of the continent's great migratory paths, the Central Flyway. Ten percent of North America's two thousand species of birds breed here; another ten percent come through on routes carrying them farther north. The state hosts more than one hundred fifty species of songbirds alone.

Central Dakota's sloughs and pondlets provide ideal breeding conditions for countless birds — pelicans and avocets, mallards and great blue herons, pintails and cormorants, blue-winged teals and snow geese, sandhill cranes and phalaropes and many mores.

Ornithologists, precise in their discipline, have placed the number of the state's visiting and resident birds at fifty-three million per year. Perhaps an equal number pass overhead, dipping down only for the night during their journeys. The numbers are equally credible to hunters thrilled by the sight of a slough peppered with mallards and canvasbacks, and farmers horrified at swarms of blackbirds settling on their sunflowers.

Yet that winged population, huge as it seems, is almost surely a fraction of what the region once supported. Professional hunters took their toll of gamebirds after they had finished off the buffalo. The prairie chicken (properly, the pinnated grouse) was threatened with extinction until the 1913 Legislature passed a law banning the commercial sale of wild game.

The antagonism between the wild and the cultivated makes farming a menace to many kinds of birdlife by its very nature. Brushy cover is plowed under. Potholes and marshes are drained. Chemicals in recent years have added other obstacles for birdlife.

What's progress in agriculture is frequently disaster for wildlife. By the same token, what's a cash crop for the farmer is often viewed as breakfast by a bird.

An aggressive program of preserving wetlands for breeding habitat has led to widespread public land acquisition throughout the heartland region. Farmers, too, have planted trees and maintained wetlands to encourage wildlife conservation. Today a larger proportion of land is set aside for wildlife preservation in North Dakota than in any other state.

The U.S. Fish and Wildlife Service and the North Dakota Game and Fish Department maintain a number of refuges throughout the prairie pothole country. Their efforts to maintain and increase populations of threatened species have led to a number of successes, especially the restoration of giant Canada geese once thought to be extinct.

The sloughs and lakes of central North Dakota have been recognized as North America's greatest waterfowl factory since the days before statehood. Public policy seems to insure that, for now, ducks and geese can sleep secure. (Whether the same can be true for the farmers who help support them remains a matter of eternal doubt.)

Sportsmen have taken advantage of the region's prolific gamebirds since well before statehood. Many a pioneer's table was graced by roast goose or duck or grouse; the introduction of the ring-necked pheasant, an Asian native, in 1910 would pave the way for meat on country tables during the meager depressed Dirty '30s.

Proud duck hunters displayed the product of a single day's sport after a jaunt afield near Webster, Dakota Territory.

Locomotives pulled private hunting cars from Chicago and Saint Paul during the years just before and after statehood, carrying the riflemen and their bird dogs to choice locales where they could bag their limits in gentlemanly style. One such aristocratic marksman was the artist Frederic Remington, who was persuaded to join an expedition to central North Dakota scarcely two years after the state had joined the Union. He shot prairie chickens in wheat stubble near Valley City and blue-winged teal and snow geese in the sloughs near Devils Lake, all en route to the Badlands for elk and cowboy adventures.

"As the sun sank, the flight of ducks began, and from the far corners of the marsh I saw puffs of smoke and heard the dull slump of a report," he later wrote in Harper's Monthly. "... The air was now full of flying birds — mallards, spoonbills, pintails, redheads, butterballs, gadwalls, widgeon and canvasbacks — and the shooting was fast and furious."

"It was a perfect revelry of slaughter. The sun has set, and no longer bathes the landscape in its golden light, and yet I sit in the water and mud and indulge this pleasurable taste for gore, wondering why it all is so ecstatic."

Hunters and fishermen found that prairie pothole country provided almost unbelievable bounty in its early days of settlement. The Forman Gun Club, above, poses with waterfowl bagged in 1908; Nelson County hunters Hutchinson and Metcalf display similar results in the 1890s (far left). The six anglers took their fish from the Sheyenne River at about the same time.

Geese rise, thick as a cloud of mosquitoes, above a cornfield near Oakes (above), while gulls track a Medina area farmer's progress (left). Denizens of the pothole country's refuges at right include a swan and her cygnets, giant Canada geese, pelicans, a snow goose and a flurry of waterfowl.

Potholes maintained by conservation-minded farmers and sheltered preserves like the Upper Souris Wildlife Refuge and many others provide the breeding ground for much of North America's waterfowl population, leading to the region's popular designation as "America's Duck Factory."

Watersport thrives in central and northern North Dakota in contrast with the region's unpredictable semi-arid climate. A walleye fishermen's success is matched by youngsters catching trout (above) on Gravel Lake. Wildlife management officials net fish on the Upper Souris Refuge at left. Right, Devils Lake sailors race in the annual Creel Cup Regatta.

Youngsters fish from a bridge downstream from the Federal Fish Hatchery north of Valley City, one of several major fish-producing operations supplying fingerlings to waters in North Dakota and other states. Water skiers (bottom) skim the surface of Devils Lake.

Children emerge from the water of Devils Lake at Arrowhead Resort — a benefit of the inexplicable freshening and rising of the land-locked lake. It had shrunk far from its original shoreline and become intensely saturated with salt and other minerals in the middle years of the century. Below, so-called "pike grass" hints of lurking northerns.

Herds of bison once shook the earth of the northern prairie. Today remnants remain at Sully's Hill Federal Game Refuge. Deer, on the other hand, have thrived along with agriculture.

Fort Totten (left) hosts one of the region's largest pow wows each July.

Crossing Over

Eric Sevareid was speaking of his state's image, not its history, when he summed up his boyhood impression of North Dakota as "a large, rectangular blank spot in the nation's mind."

But the Velva-born newsman was echoing an historic theme as well. The center of North Dakota played that role for more than half of its recorded past. As the Missouri River became a thoroughfare and the Red River drew early settlement south, the heart of the prairie remained a land in waiting. It was country to cross over.

To the modern Indian tribes who mastered it, and to the polyglot procession of adventurers, traders and soldiers who followed in their wake, the northern edge of the Great Plains seemed as daunting in its emptiness as any geographic obstacle — as formidable, in its whispering featureless terrain and oddly terrorizing quiet, as the most violent river or tortured mountain range.

Movement was the drift prairie's principal theme. It was the way Sioux tribes coped with their new life in open country in the 1700s after the Chippewa had harried them west from Minnesota's forests.

It was the strategy of Nor'Westers and the men of Hudson's Bay, traveling across its emptiness to trade with the Mandan and Hidatsa villages of the Upper Missouri River.

It was the means by which early French, British, and American explorers tested its distance in the quest for a northwest passage to the Pacific Ocean. They were searching less for this land's potential than for a quicker way across.

That momentum carried the Northern Pacific Railroad and, later, the Great Northern across the prairie. Though towns were tossed out rapidly in their wake — Valley City and Jamestown on the N.P. mainline, Devils Lake and Minot along James J. Hill's

G.N. tracks — they were at first incidental to the transcontinental goal.

Only when less remote, more reassuring acres had been consumed by settlement did central North Dakota's moment come, beginning late in the nineteenth century and lasting well into the twentieth. Except for river-valley farmers and a few towns planted squarely astride the rails, most of the central and northern parts of upper Dakota Territory remained an empty cross-over country until well after North Dakota entered the Union.

History has underlined one point: The high, wide center of North America has rarely been a first choice. Those who have drawn its lot have learned to adapt and, in the process, have won an unexpected prize. Time and again, they have melded old ways and new ideas into a self-sufficient, independent life equal to the challenges that the land has thrown out.

That was the story of the Sioux, who came to control the heart of the prairie when a United States was still a novel democratic notion.

First choice had been the sheltered lakelands. When that avenue was closed off by warfare with other native American peoples, tribes of the Sioux crossed the Red River and continued moving west, leaving behind the relative luxury of woodlands for the rigors of the open plains.

They adapted to the new country, as white pioneers would again be forced to learn two centuries later. The Indians sailed onto the prairie as nomads and hunters, flowing with the tide of buffalo that provisioned them. Their culture mirrored the herd's movements: across the prairie as lush spring turned into arid summer, and then

A Metis family poses with one of the ubiquitous Red River carts along the northern border in 1883. The Metis' ancestry was predominantly Chippewa and French.

down to the shelter of river valleys to dodge the winter wind.

What was a good life became better through the avenue of prairie commerce. Indian groups were trading among themselves long before white merchants claimed the territory. During trade fairs like the annual gathering hosted by Teton Sioux on the James River, the northern tribes bartered buffalo hides and meat for two special acquisitions — horses, traded north from tribe to tribe after being introduced in Mexico; and rifles, carried west by distant bands who had closer contact with white settlement.

White traders from Canada canvassed the territory from the 1780s until the War of 1812. Their principal goal was the Missouri River villages. The open prairie presented a dangerous course of passage. They zigzagged from forts in present-day Manitoba by way of the Souris River and the Turtle Mountains, then hurried south to the dubious shelter of Dodgen Butte (near the modern town of Butte) where the Sioux sometimes lay in ambush, and finally west to the water.

Trade continued in the decades which followed, centering on the Missouri River post of Fort Union, near where Williston was later founded, and the Knife River post, Fort Clark. But it slackened as the twin tragedies of smallpox and the dwindling bison herds threatened the Indians' way of life.

In later years, North Dakotans would perpetually complain that their lives were directed by powerful interests far beyond their own state's border . . . a claim as easy to prove as it has been difficult to redress.

No Dakotans have a stronger case than the Indians, whose lives were dramatically altered by the irresistible force of America's thrust to the west. The violence that wracked the central prairie during the 1860s — a bitter prelude to the settlement that would follow — was foreordained by that pressure.

The year 1862 was a watershed, with events squeezing North Dakota's destiny from both sides. On the one hand, a gold rush brought wagon trains of fortune-hunters west from St. Paul. On the other, Indians fleeing the scene of the Minnesota Massacre drew the U.S. Army west in full force under Generals Henry Hastings Sibley and Alfred Sully.

The most violent episodes in North Dakota's history followed in their wake, along with a dramatic acceleration of the U.S. Army's presence on the northern prairie. Only one fort, Abercrombie, stood at the beginning of the decade — an anchor for the trade route between early Winnipeg and St. Paul. By the end of the decade a string of fortifications stretched west.

The Army provided guides for Montana-bound expeditions setting out from Fort Abercrombie, and development of new forts was funded by a special congressional appropriation. Fort Rice went up on the Missouri in 1864, followed by Forts Ransom, Totten, Stevenson, and Buford, a series of way stations dividing the dangerous journey into somewhat-safer laps.

But events in Minnesota inspired retribution long before the forts could be built

Troops parade in full dress uniform at Fort Seward in 1894. Sioux women — dressed too in their best finery — stand before their tipis on the Fort Totten Indian Reservation.

and garrisoned. Settlement of western Minnesota had strained the patience of the Santee Sioux. A decade earlier they had given up lands in Minnesota and Iowa in return for the promised annual payments. When neither gold nor provisions were forthcoming they rebelled, killing several hundred white settlers along the Minnesota River. Fugitive Sioux fled northwestward into Dakota Territory with the Army on their trail.

Leading 2,800 men, Sibley set out in 1863 for Devils Lake, where many of the Sioux had fled after the uprising. Sully headed up-river on the Missouri with 2,000 troops to cut off the Indians' escape.

Sibley's route (roughly paralleling U.S. Highway 10) led to three battles that summer with Sioux hunting parties almost certainly innocent of the deaths for which he intended retribution. The first was at Big Mound (not far from Tappen); the second, Dead Buffalo Lake (at Dawson); and the third, Stony Lake (near Driscoll). The Indian death toll was estimated at 150; survivors escaped across the Missouri.

But as Sibley returned to the Minnesota post, the Indians too returned to resume their summer's hunt along the James River. There the Sully party found them in early autumn, encamped at Whitestone Hill.

Theirs was the bloodiest battle ever fought in North Dakota. The Sioux were hunters, not warriors, accompanied by their families and burdened with a winter's stock of buffalo meat and supplies. The soldiers killed 150 men, women, and children as they tried to flee, and took an equal number captive. They burned half a million pounds of meat and some 300 lodges.

Most of the forts built in the years that followed and the troopers who manned them saw little action. They suffered more from the territorial guarantees of loneliness and hard weather than from still-volatile relations between the Sioux and the U.S.A.

The moves and countermoves of Plains Indians and Army known as the Indian Wars had been set into motion on the northern plains. A dozen years later they would culminate in the battle of the Little Big Horn. In the meantime there were skirmishes here and there, peaces made and peaces broken, uncertainty over claims and rights, and a potential surge of settlers knocking at the door waiting for the land to be opened to homestead.

Treaty established a Sioux reservation on the south shore of Devils Lake in the winter before carpenters began building Fort Totten. Later the local bands were joined by Indians from the Souris River who settled nearby, originally attracted by government food rations. They had been starving. The once-bountiful prairie had been hunted nearly bare.

For many years Chippewas and Metis continued to claim the land northwest of Devils Lake and the Fort Totten reservation — an area also eagerly eyed by white settlers who arrived too late to homestead or purchase acreage in the Red River Valley. Eventually most of the Metis accepted offers of individual allotments of land. Some 25 families of full-blooded Chippewa chose instead to settle on the new Turtle Mountain Reservation, established in 1884 in Rolette County.

Mail routes were laid out and maintained from Abercrombie to Montana, traced as well by drovers hauling provisions for the soldiers and tiny civilian populations clinging to their forts.

The lonely crossings were not quite over yet in the Dakota outland. But with the heart of the prairie finally secure, and with the railroads still to come, prospects of settlement began to emerge at last as not too wild a dream.

General Sibley

General Sully

Memories of early forts remain vivid. Fort Totten (above, in 1878) continues to look much as it once did, though trees have grown to shade its avenues and square. The Fort Seward Historical Museum marks the site of the former fort, dismantled long ago. A monument mounted on a hill high above the surrounding prairie commemorates Sibley's soldiers who died in the Battle of Whitestone Hill; a much smaller stone cairn at its foot was raised in 1942 to memorialize the 150 Sioux men, women and children killed in the conflict.

Preserved as a state historic site, Fort Totten offers visitors a glimpse of life in what is widely considered to be the best-preserved military fort of the Indian Wars period.

Today North Dakotans recreate frontier days with authentically outfitted units of a new Seventh Cavalry. Companies from Fort Ransom, Fort Buford and Fort Seward here reenact scenes from military life in a summer encampment.

Pow wows like the traditional summer contest at Fort Totten preserve traditional music, dancing and fellowship among Indian nations of the plains and woodlands. Their heritage reaches back beyond the coming of white traders and settlers, when they provided a festive opportunity for trade among tribes.

Roman Catholic missionaries played an important role in family and community life on the Fort Totten Reservation. The mission church at St. Michael was a center not only of worship but of education and fellowship, introducing early reservation residents to white customs and culture.

Modern Indian people carry on an old honored tradition, the Sun Dance, on the Turtle Mountain Reservation. The deeply spiritual ceremony asks for the guidance of the Great Spirit.

Contemporary life revolves around employment at reservation-based industries like Devils Lake Sioux Manufacturing (opposite, above), a military subcontractor; Four Winds School at Fort Totten, and a modern money-making innovation, Dacotah Bingo in the now-empty St. Michael school.

Shortly after winning a national book award for *Love Medicine* Louise Erdrich was interviewed in North Dakota *Horizon* Magazine.

Her thoughts are always close to her homeland. She says that her experiences growing up in North Dakota formed her as writer. When she accepted her award in New York, she did so "in the spirit of the Turtle Mountains and of North Dakota ... m inspiration really started early on with my parents and with m husband."

As a child she was always among storytellers. She becam intrigued with the family tales passed on by her German fathe from Minnesota and her Chippewa mother from the Turtle Mou tain Reservation, where Erdrich is also an enrolled member of th Chippewa tribe. Her heritage became a vital part of her ow identity at an early age, but she did not realize its relevance impact until she began writing.

Here is an excerpt from *Love Medicine* describing a drive fro Fargo to Rolla:

Driving north, I could see the earth lifting. The wind was ho and smelled of tar and the moving dust.

At the end of the big farms and the blowing fields was the rese vation. I always knew it was coming a long way off. Even in th distance you sense hills from their opposites — pits, dried slough ditches or cattails, potholes. And then the water. There would b water in the hills when there wasn't any on the plains, because th hollows saved it, collected runoff from the low slopes, and th dense trees held it, too. I thought of water in the roots of trees brown and bark smelling, cold.

Author Louise Erdrich has won national attention for he writings about North Dakota life, with Indian character playing the central roles. The native of Wahpeton, enrolled member of the Turtle Mountain Band o Chippewa, earned major prizes including a National Boo Award for **Love Medicine,** *her first novel.*

Sculptor Leo Wilkie of Dunseith interprets Ojibway (Chippewa) culture and beliefs through his carvings in stone and wood and through his visits with schoolchildren. He credits his people's sensitivity to nature with the essential ability of the artist to see the beauty present all around him.

One hundred years ago the wagon trains carved ruts across the prairie which can still be seen in spots today. But more remains of their tradition of hard-working, hot, dusty travel. Each summer the Fort Seward Wagon Train sets out over the central North Dakota sod, recreating pioneer ways for modern "tenderfeet" more accustomed to air conditioning and microwave ovens than jouncing in an open wagon and cooking stew over a campfire.

The Northern Pacific reached Crystal Springs in 1873, where a town was founded a decade later. Above, the Great Northern Hotel of Devils Lake marks the competing rail line's dominance in the northern tier.

Coming Home

To trace a prairie city's family tree, just follow the tracks and the branch lines.

The lineage of all of North Dakota's major towns and most of their smaller cousins is as simple as can be: They are the natural offspring of Mother Nature and a railroad train.

Nature got here first with her open horizon and a feisty climate perfectly paired to grow endless grain and fatten herds of cattle. Many were already traditional local crossroads at choice spots along the banks of prairie rivers.

But real excitement came to northern Dakota Territory with the hoot and rumble of a locomotive... the sound of a lean and empty land poised to sprout the budding contours of its future.

Beneath the rich counterpoint of exploration and adventure, modern North Dakota owes its creation almost solely to the railroads. Nowhere is that parental obligation more clear than in its central and its northern counties.

Scarce indeed is the city or village without a Great Northern or a Northern Pacific or a Soo Line in its past. The family resemblance is unmistakable in the profile each displays from a distance. A grain elevator juts perpendicular to the parallel trackage, sure indication that this marks the spot where the wheat yields of the early farms were siphoned off for the mills of Minneapolis, and where the contemporary harvest still frequently meets its markets.

Back east, where settlements were older and more steady on their roots, the pattern was different. The railroads came along to serve the towns. They angled their lines accordingly like a connect-the-dots puzzle, sketching out a broader picture between predetermined points.

Here the rails crossed first. Their long, straight lines were directed toward a farther object — the Pacific shore of Puget Sound, the copper mines of Montana. Only afterward were towns added as punctuation.

The northern territory's major cities emerged where iron rails encountered water. Valley City was born where the Northern Pacific crossed the Sheyenne River and Jamestown on the James River. A dozen years later, as the Great Northern (then known as the St. Paul, Minneapolis and Manitoba Railroad) pressed westward, two which Jim Hill predicted would become "good towns" were certain bets — one located on Devils Lake and borrowing its name, the other, Minot, on the Souris River. (The same would be true of Dickinson when the N.P. reached the Heart River, and Williston when Hill's railway touched the Missouri.)

Civic foundings followed the railroads' progress. The Northern Pacific reached from Fargo to Bismarck in 1872 and 1873. Settlements along its mainline tended to celebrate their centennials in the 1970s, with the festivities working their way westward year by year.

The Great Northern moved across the state a decade later. Its progress in the 1880s is mirrored by simultaneous anniversaries observed across both south and north central counties as Hill built his main road and several branch lines.

The oldest towns along the N.P. had shaky beginnings in the early 1870s. Not until the beginning of the Great Dakota Boom in 1878 did settlement really begin to blossom west of the Red River Valley. A number of townsites were platted at attractive sites directly on the railroad, yet failed to catch hold until the economy quickened and touched off the boom.

The Great Northern's timing was better. Its progress was steady through the following years — to Devils Lake by 1883 and Minot in 1886, followed by a break-neck construction season that reached Great Falls in 1887. At the same time, branches were being built west from Grand Forks to Neche, from Wahpeton to Ellendale and across the western Red River Valley.

Thousands of men laid track across the prairie during the Great Northern's full-throttle drive toward the west in 1887.

The advance of the railways spurred intense curiosity and excitement. That towns would thrive at trackside was a foregone conclusion... but precisely where the rails would pass was a matter of high intrigue.

Promoters purchased scraps of bare prairie acreage and christened them with often grandiose names — New Chicago, New Minneapolis, Gwynne City, Wamduska, LaFollette. They longed to lure the railroads to the Main Streets and Broadways platted optimistically across buffalo grass and bluestem.

At the same time, they laid claim to prosperous futures in lavish newspaper advertisements directed at potential residents. They trolled for incoming businessmen and professionals with exemplary bravado, promising that those who took up their invitation would become the "first families" of a glorious new urban center.

But the railroads rarely responded as townsite promoters desired. The Northern Pacific employed its own developers, while the Great Northern was associated with several other firms, including one in which Hill himself owned a substantial interest.

Their closely guarded plans served their own purposes. Fine points of routings were often settled to avoid, rather than accommodate, would-be boomtowns lying in wait for locomotives. While sites controlled by the railroad's stockholders and insiders were graced with tracks, those promoted by outside boosters lost hope and shriveled just a few miles away.

These losers in the siting schemes came to be known as "inland towns" — marooned not far from water, but from rails.

James J. Hill addresses residents of Williston in 1909. The city was an outpost of his magnificent vision of the Northwest's potential for development.

The American recession of the 1890s put further railroad expansion in hiatus. But they resumed their strategy when better times returned: Build lines across this promising, still-empty land, and then develop towns to gather a section of the farming hinterland into their sphere. There grain elevators — owned or controlled by the railroads themselves — would produce freight traffic to keep the steam engines tugging wheat-filled cars toward the mills of Minneapolis.

During the 1800s the Northern Pacific and Great Northern informally divided North Dakota between them to minimize direct competition. Despite their deal, the N.P.'s finances remained shaky. When it was declared bankrupt in 1893, Hill said his cronies acquired the reins through their purchase of stock, leaving Hill in control of four-fifths of North Dakota's rail miles.

But another of his decisions inspired head-to-head battle on a different front. The Canadian Pacific Railway acquired the St. Paul, Minneapolis and Sault St. Marie Railroad — the Soo Line — in 1888, anticipating that Hill's eastbound carloads of wheat would be transported in turn by their line to eastern ports beyond Minneapolis. Hill declined, choosing a Chicago route instead.

And so the Canadian-controlled Soo set out to challenge his reign over the very territory where he had won the nickname of "Empire Builder." It constructed a diagonal route from Hankinson to Portal in the 1890s; in 1905 it came even closer to the heart of his empire with its Wheat Line from Kenmare to Thief River Falls, MN.

A new crop of towns, Soo towns, began to pop up on the plains. Their establishment, paralleling railroad progress, continued well into the period known as the Second Dakota Boom.

A renewed burst of railroad-building coincided with the Soo's enthusiasm for North Dakota. Both major carriers and newcomers added thousands of miles of track. Among the smaller lines was the Chicago, Milwaukee and St. Paul — the Milwaukee Road — which sent a branch north from South Dakota to Strasburg and Linton. Wheatgrowers even developed trackage of their own in enterprises like the Farmers Grain and Shipping Company of Ramsey County, which built a line from Devils Lake to Starkweather and Hansboro.

This late spate of town-founding finally carried settlement deep into the rolling semi-arid hills of south central North Dakota and the high plains of the state's northwest quadrant.

A web of rails criss-crossed central and northern North Dakota by the beginning of World War I. The tally of townsites had multiplied accordingly.

Business boomed in many quarters, matching for awhile the grandiose future which Hill and his colleagues had foretold for the northwest. General stores, banks, churches and still-illicit saloons proliferated at an unlikely rate. Streets bustled with farmers hauling grain and cattle or shopping for supplies.

Immigrants worked at mastering the American language as they plowed farms of their own, the land of which they'd dreamed. Townspeople created a veneer of culture in towns where boulevards were lined with saplings the size of broomsticks. Schoolbells rang, and politicians delivered patriotic oratory, and bands were played on Sundays in new parks.

The picture was still far from perfect. Farmers complained bitterly of railroad freight rates and manipulation by the economic interests of Minneapolis. Families newly arrived from the Old County suffered sometimes-horrible deprivations as they adjusted to a new nation and learned to farm its fields. Not all dreams, in town as well as the country, could stand up in the brilliant unshadowed light of the prairie day.

But the railroads steamed along fresh-laid tracks across their distant domain, and small-town life bustled at the heart of the prairie. Many North Dakota towns would never know better times than these.

These were the good old days.

Grand optimism of the early days is reflected in the elaborate Kirkwood House of Carrington, built in 1896; and the five grain elevators along the tracks in Esmond, which boasted of their combined capacity of 350,000 bushels.

Northern Pacific High-Line Bridge, Valley City.

Gassman Coulee west of Minot (upper left) presented Great Northern engineers with a major grade to vanquish. Flat rails trail northwest in the sunset north of Kenmare. An engineer with Burlington Northern — the merged offspring of the Great Northern and Northern Pacific lines — pauses in Aneta.

Railroads have carried the prairie's products to market through bumper years and bad. Grain is loaded in a Soo Line car at Fullerton while the coal tipple at Larson in Burke County reflects declining demand for its lignite.

Rural Main Streets have felt the effects of changing times and travel patterns, like these in Bowbells (left) and Rolla. They share two common elements in their stability — railroads and county seats.

Small town life moves at its own special pace. Children park their bikes for baseball in Velva, a town known for its strength in sports. A tractor fills up at the Cenex pump in Dawson, while a lone driver navigates a solitary stretch of road near Grand Rapids.

Quiet days offer special reflective moments in central North Dakota — a watery mirror in Petersburg, a family pedalling together in Steele, friends cantering down a side street in Tappen.

"Going to town" is still an occasion of note for the chance to socialize as well as to conduct commerce. Main street businesses like Peterson's Grocery in Carpio (top left) and those of downtown Crosby are centers for neighborly greetings. So are establishments like the Old West Tavern in Mapes and, on a larger scale, the Chieftain Motel of Carrington, scene of countless meetings because of its central location.

Small towns struggle to survive in the '80s. Pingree still welcomes infrequent travelers to its civic greenspace. The post office anchors Tuttle's business district. An unoccupied store in Sheyenne still sports the community's westernized decor, an attempt to preserve its business vitality. The culprit in many cases of decline: Good surfaced roads carrying local customers beyond them to larger markets.

LaMoure maintains its pride in its leading native son — the late U.S. Senator Milton Young, known for decades as "Mr. Wheat;" below, a local yard sports a patriotic motif. The post office occupies a former hotel in Eldridge, one of the few structures which remain. Basketball — here, a contest pitting the North Central High School girls team against area rivals — draws most of the community to the Rogers gymnasium. The consolidated district also serves Dazey and Sanborn.

The school and post office still stand, abandoned, in Arena, a town platted in 1910 which has disappeared from most modern maps. Other reminders of even earlier settlement are scattered across the central North Dakota countryside, like this once-snug log cabin nestled in the valley of the Sheyenne River north of Fort Ransom.

The decline of a small town means the end, not only to enterprises like the Verendrye store (at left), but to an entire range of institutions. Yet optimism continues to fuel the hopes of dedicated local supporters like the proprietor of Sheyenne's Farmers and Merchants Bank. His building displays the brave legend, "Nothing was ever lost through an abiding faith in North Dakota."

Memorials to the Germans from Russia — an empty sod house along Highway 13 and iron crosses in the Wishek cemetery.

From Fjords and Steppes to the Prairie

When North Dakota joined the Union in 1889, it carried a distinction it would claim for years to come: From coast to coast, it could boast the largest proportion of citizens who were imported.

Forty-three percent of North Dakotans had been born overseas or in Canada by the year of statehood. First- and second-generation Americans made up better than two-thirds of the new state's population.

Twenty years later, when the railroads had nearly finished their iron web, the distinction not only remained intact... it was even more dramatic. According to historian Elwyn Robinson, more than one in four North Dakotans of 1910 had been born in another nation. They and their children counted for 71 percent of the total.

The ethnic makeup of those first generations of Dakotans reflected railroad progress and the western edge of the last homestead land available in the United States. But it also mirrors greater events overseas. The great historical events that marked European history in the nineteenth century would leave their mark on the heart of the prairie, half a planet away.

Over-population, famine, religious movements and international politics all sent waves of immigrants washing over North America.

At the eve of the state's modern history, far-off developments affected the region only in conflicting claims by the French, English and Spanish crowns and skirmishes between traders opening the hinterland. It lay silent for a century while turbulent tides of distant politics waxed and waned.

By statehood, though, their tug had become very real. The East and Mideast had been filled by successive movements of people from the British Isles and elsewhere in western Europe. As the ethnic waves continued over the years, they were beached on a series of new frontiers. From the 1880s through the 'teens they came overland to North Dakota.

The railroads, so much a mainstay of North Dakota's development, played their usual role in attracting immigration. Northern Pacific agents began their no-holds-barred campaign in 1879. It continued for a decade, magnified past the turn of the century by the Great Northern's even more aggresive initiative to populate James J. Hill's personal vision of a bountiful and prosperous Northwest.

Dakota Territory and, later, the new state added their voices to the clamor, playing off hopes of the unsatisfied in eastern America and abroad. Even Canada drew settlers to northern North Dakota with advertising meant to bring pioneers to its own western wheatlands. Substantial numbers of Canadian recruits drifted south of the border and took up claims in northwestern North Dakota.

Not all of the foreign-born men and women who responded to the boosters' sales pitch came from abroad. Many arrived on their second bounce across the United States, settling first in the Midwest and then moving on as new lands opened to homestead.

Nor, of course, was this the last move for many. Countless homesteaders and townspeople settled the central and northern counties but continued on. Drawn here by promised opportunity, they were disappointed by a stringent reality of marginal farms and towns with stunted growth. Yet they could still believe, and went on to follow other Pied Pipers closer to the sea.

And so a population already strong in northern and central Europeans became distilled to an even higher concentration as hardy Scandinavians and Germans purchased land left behind by less tenacious settlers.

About 15 percent of the state's people were Norwegian-born and five percent German-born at statehood. In 1910, Norwegians made up 21 percent of the population and Germans, including Germans from Russian, another 20. (The proportion of Russian-Germans continued to rise through the end of World War I, when they slightly outnumbered North Dakotans of Norse descent.)

The decades have helped fade vividness from a state in which new American citizens played so great a part. But their legacy remains, from sauerkraut and the schottische to lutefisk and that ubiquitous exclamation, "Uff da!"

Central North Dakota still carries the imprint of the Germans from Russia, whose hard work and fierce determination to build their farms wrung a living from stony fields and sometimes-unrelenting land.

The northern tier in particular remains a Scandinavian stronghold. Though Norwegians predominate, the Swedes and Danes and Icelanders and Finns are nowhere more in evidence in this state.

A German-Russian family poses in front of its sod house south of Jud at the turn of the century.

These revelers are celebrating a German-Russian wedding in Pierce County in 1915.

Large numbers of Norwegians began looking west across the Atlantic in the middle 1800s. They were inspired by the dream of holding land, the greatest aspiration for ambitious Scandinavian youth looking to better their lot.

At home over-population and inheritance customs made the dream increasingly remote. But in America there were acres aplenty on new frontiers — first in Wisconsin, Minnesota and Iowa, and then on into North Dakota.

They made their mark by their departure. In the Old Country, Norway lost fully a quarter of its population between 1850 and 1900. In the New World, Norwegians and their other Scandinavian cousins assume a dominant role in the lakelands and on the prairie.

No country could have looked less inviting to the families Jim Hill's railroads carried west. Instead of pine, they found prairie. Instead of fjords, there were potholes. Instead of mountains that sheltered cozy villages, they met only openness encircling towns where ferocious winds scoured paint from wooden storefronts.

It was natural that the Norwegians would first choose wooded land by water. The Sheyenne River was settled first as they reached beyond the Red River Valley. They kept pace as the Great Northern moved west from Devils Lake toward Bottineau and Minot and beyond. Early arrivals selected choice plots along the rivers, creeks or lakesides, leaving upland fields to be plowed by late-comers.

Many Norwegian homesteaders filed their claims as bachelors. Only after they had built their shanties and turned the sod did they send back to the Old Country for their brides or families.

Many Norwegian settlers had begun to master the language and American ways in a first encounter in Minnesota or the Midweest and fit into Dakota life with relative ease. They mingled with their neighbors, built their schools to educate their children as Americans, and blended into the fabric of North Dakota life. It was the prairie landscape itself that seemed strange and foreign.

The story of the Germans from Russia was nearly opposite. From the beginning, the prairie looked like home. But for nearly 50 years they persisted in living a life apart from the mainstream.

They clung to their language, their churches and their customs in tightly-knit enclaves and distrusted most public institutions. They were unyielding in their determination to maintain their traditional ways — the ways they had defended for the century just past in the midst of other foreigners on another continent.

Pioneering was not a new experience for the Germans from Russia, whose journey to North Dakota was the second undertaken within little more than a century. Originally farmers in Germany, they were invited to settle raw Russian land by Catherine the Great in 1760, and again in 1801 by Czar Alexander.

The offer appealed to tens of thousands of Germans. Their nation was only beginning to recover from the devastation of the Seven Years War. The Russian rules promised not only land to call their own but guarantees of political and religious independence. They could, and would, remain German even on the Volga River and the Black Sea.

The steppes of Russia were not so different from what their grandchildren would encounter in the Dakotas. The soil was often thin and rainfall erratic. Yet they valued land over all, and clung, steady and persistent, to their hard Eurasian farms for three and four generations. Despite the odds, they prospered.

Politics finally broke the connection. By the last half of the nineteenth century, Russia was no longer content with a prosperous colony of determined Germanic traditions in its midst. Past guarantees of cultural independence were breached, and German men were for the first time drafted by the Russian Army.

Scouting parties set out to find better opportunities abroad, reaching the United States at precisely the time that the central Dakotas — so like the steppes — were being opened.

The Chicago, Milwaukee and St. Paul Railroad played as great a part in bringing German-Russians to south central North Dakota as its more dominant competitors had the Norwegians and others throughout the rest of the state. Its advertising in the Ukraine inspired a steady stream of families who departed Russia for the prairie, tracing its progress across South Dakota from Yankton to Aberdeen, Ipswich and finally Eureka.

Historian William Sherman calls Eureka the "mother colony" for most of North Dakota's German-Russians. They begain arriving in 1884 by the trainload,

jumping off to find homesteads at points farther north.

They rode in wagons or hiked along a trail that led first to McIntosh County. As land was taken up, they spread to Dickey and Emmons counties and then north until they became the majority in what is now known as the German-Russian Triangle. Its base lies between Emmons and Dickey counties on the south; its apex is in McHenry, Pierce and Bottineau.

Religion was an organizing principle behind the towns they founded. Like the settlements in Russia they left behind, the German-Russians established North Dakota colonies which were thoroughly Protestant or thoroughly Catholic in their worship. The pattern of pioneer days still remains firmly entrenched across central North Dakota.

Though Norwegians and German-Russians are the dominant strains in today's blend of North Dakotans, other traditions have added their special flavors to contemporary life.

The first settlers to follow the Indians, French and Metis into the northern and central regions were eastern Americans. Some came to carve out new lives in the years after the Civil War. Others were simply looking for a chance to make their fortune.

British, Scottish and Irish names are prominent, too, in early Dakota annals. Germans came from Europe or from older American settlements. Danes, Swedes, Icelanders and Finns are scattered throughout the region, along with smaller numbers of Ukrainians, Syrians, Bohemians, Poles, Hollanders and Belgians. Sherman records past settlements as well of Jews, Gypsies, Japanese and Black Americans — gone today, but once evidence of either the deep attraction of land at the heart of the contininent, or the well-oiled skill of salesmen who told glorious tales of its potential.

The diversity of early days has steadily diminished. Many tried, and failed, to tame the heart of the prairie. While their sturdier neighbors consumed the land they left behind, their tradition remains — an unexpected, half-overlooked and bittersweet reminder of the tremendous power of dreams touched by splendid advertising.

Germans from Russia at first resisted American ways, just as they had resisted Russianization in the years before. In this 1930s photo, men wait their turn to vote for the first North Dakota politician to earn their active support, maverick William Langer. Above, the Mueller homestead northwest of Kulm was photographed in 1894.

Long-established congregations trace the ethnic backgrounds of early North Dakotans. Fort Ransom's Lutheran church (above) marks an area of Norwegian settlement. Lakota's lovely stone Episcopal church speaks of the Anglo-American and Yankee townspeople prominent at the beginning of local history. Michigan's United Church of Christ congregation celebrated its centennial in 1883. Less religious early Dakotans often formed secular groups like Lidgerwood's ZCBJ Lodge, established in 1897; it is now owned by the Knights of Columbus.

Now scattered around the country, past and present members of Denbigh Lutheran church gather to celebrate their congregation's hundredth birthday and (at right) to pose for a "family" portrait by well-wisher Bill Snyder. The nearby cemetery includes the grave of one member of particular note, Norwegian ski hero Sondre Norheim, who emigrated at the age of 59 to homestead in the Denbigh area.

Music speaks in the language of immigrant heritages at the annual Fiddler's Jamboree each July at the International Peace Garden. Grandparents revel in the crowd's appreciation of their down-home virtuosity, and share their love of the great old tunes and traditions with a young and nimble-fingered generation.

The labor and laughter of old-time threshing is kept alive at annual threshing bees across central North Dakota — from Makoti and New Rockford to here in Fort Ransom. Veterans of the pre-combine era stoke the steam engines and feed bundles of swathed grain into the rumbling and clanking machines, which pour out fine streams of grain and belching clouds of smoke and golden chaff in equal proportion. A rank of salvaged machines stand at attention on the grounds of the Divide County Museum at Crosby (right).

Historical societies take loving care of prized possessions and everyday artifacts from the pioneer era — here, at the LaMoure County Museum near Grand Rapids and the Stutsman County Museum in Jamestown. Descendants of Norse immigrants show personal pride in their heritage in a host of ways, from authentic Norwegian bunads (the national dress) to special recipes for favorite delicacies taught by mother to daughter across the years.

The North Dakota Winter Show, held each March in Valley City, has enlivened the past 50 winters for rural families across the state. Besides its famous livestock competitions, it features displays of hobbies, crafts and good home cooking with an ethnic twist.

Minot's Hostefest celebrates the Nordic heritage shared by much of northern North Dakota. Besides music, good eating and settlement-era crafts kept alive by second- and third-generation Americans, it draws headliners like accordian virtuoso Myron Floren.

Reunions bring together the scattered natives of North Dakota's towns and cities — whether a family farm centennial, a civic birthday party, or a school or church jubilee. Shown here are the Quick family farm centennial near Dazey, a street dance during Minot's centennial, and a Karlsruhe man enjoying the lavish potluck menu inevitably featured during get-togethers.

Two Great Northern towns, Grenora (left) and Minot, have met widely divergent fates.

Surge of the Cities

In the beginning of prairie settlement, all things seemed possible...all civic dreams within their founders' grasp.

Some of those dreams lived brief and futile lives. Some flourished for 30 years, or 20, or 10, and then withered to tiny, static landmarks fighting to maintain their place on the map.

And some — like those envisioned by their founders as "good towns" in the heart of the prairie — did come to match or mirror the hopes with which they were christened. They started well and weathered setbacks.

Today the central and northern counties are arranged in market areas around the dominant towns of Minot, Devils Lake, Valley City and Jamestown, and in smaller circles around the second rank of cities. They salute dynamic founders when centennials roll around, but keep in mind another factor in their growth: a smile from Lady Luck.

Winners and losers in the great civic sifting-out were evident from the very start. They could be sorted by the endowments on which they had been built; an objective observer, of which there were precious few among the boomers, could already see the shape of things to come.

The settlements that would become the most vigorous cities shared a number of blessings. First and foremost was their railroad lineage.

Not only did the rails intersect with pleasant rivers or lakeshores near the Main Streets they laid out. Each also briefly sampled the status of terminus of the tracks. Until construction moved once again onto the trackless prairie, they savored a moment as the last jumping-off point on the great migration west. It was a boon for nearby homesteaders, a lure for pioneer merchants, and a setting in which the vanguard of American civilization could sink tentative roots.

But the hoot of locomotives was only part of the natural harmony that led Minot, Valley City, Jamestown and Devils Lake to their regional dominance, and inspired parallels on a smaller scale among their mid-sized cousins.

The water that lapped at their front doors had its own significance. In an often-thirsty land, ready fresh water was an asset worth the price it extracted in sometimes-disastrous spring floods.

And water, too, meant trees. Another scarce commodity, they were more than a luxury for plains-weary eyes. The cottonwoods and elms and burr oaks along Devils Lake and the Souris, James and Sheyenne Rivers offered a limited supply of timbers for log cabins and, later, local lumber mills. They provided clean, sweet-smelling fuel made more desirable by the region's memories of campfires stoked with dried buffalo dung. They offered shelter as well, both physical and emotional, arming their settlers with defense against the howling vagaries of harsh seasons at the center of the continent.

Each of the winners in the city-building sweepstakes boasted a valuable gift from the canny politicking of the frenzied years before statehood: It was created a county seat or captured the designation.

The impact of county government has been blurred across decades of good highways, fast cars and instant electronic communication. Its original pride can still be glimpsed in the regal courthouses that rise above county seats, built when the designation was central to the ambitions of town developers.

Squabbles and violent outbursts mark the histories of a number of central and northern towns. Typical was the political scuffling in LaMoure County a century ago, when the city of LaMoure managed to wres-

Kenmare's Danish heritage was reflected in the pastimes of an earlier day, like ice-boating on Middle Des Lacs Lake.

tle county government away from Grand Rapids five years after its founding in 1881.

Both towns had railroad lines. Both were on the banks of the James River. During its brief heyday Grand Rapids was the prouder sight. But after the courthouse had been relocated to LaMoure, the trend was all too clear. One hundred years later, LaMoure residents number more than 1,000 — respectable and progressive among rural North Dakota cities. Grand Rapids is a virtual ghost town.

Political clout had other rewards, too, right from the start. The trading and re-trading of favors during the original constitutional convention in 1889 created state institutions in central North Dakota's leading cities, as the king-makers of the statehood era liberally salted them with high-minded enterprises to secure their support.

First among them was Jamestown, an avid contender itself for the territorial capital back in 1883. (It would renew its quixotic campaign again in the early 1930s, after the original Bismarck structure had burned down, but voters would turn down its offer by an enormous margin.) The territorial legislature established "a hospital for the care of the insane" there in 1884. Its claim was reaffirmed in the state's constitution.

The constitutionally-mandated State School of Forestry was established in the Turtle Mountains at Bottineau in 1907. Today it is affiliated with North Dakota State University.

The constitution distributed other plums as well, among them Valley City State College (originally a normal school and then a teachers college), the State School of Forestry at Bottineau (now a branch of North Dakota State University), and the Ellendale Industrial and Normal School. Devils Lake became the site of the School for the Deaf, and the Old Soldiers' Home was slated for Lisbon.

Two other institutions were added in later years. The normal school which evolved into Minot State College was mandated in 1913. At Dunseith, the State Tuberculosis Sanitarium cared for victims of the disease during the period in which it was a major public health threat; later the campus of San Haven was allied with the State School for the Retarded at Grafton for care of the most severly handicapped residents.

The Presbyterian Church fostered Jamestown College, which weathered difficult times and a 16-year hiatus before emerging as a small but respected liberal arts institution. Northwest Bible College was established in Minot. Just a decade ago Trinity Bible College moved onto the Ellendale campus of the former Industrial and Teachers College, which had been partly destroyed by fire and subsequently closed. Devils Lake moved into higher education, too, with establishment of Lake Region Community College. The two-year junior college and vocational school is presently allied with the State School of Science.

Railroads inspired the surge of the cities, but their progress after World War I was equally fueled by gasoline.

Automobiles were a novelty in the years before the war. Their popularity was limited not only by the expense, but also by the lack of decent roads. By the 1920s, though, cars and trucks had emerged as the pre-eminent shapers of the fortunes of prairie towns.

Two major transcontinental highways brought traffic to Jamestown, Valley City, Devils Lake and Minot — U.S. Highway 10 in the south, paralleling the Northern Pacific tracks, and U.S. 2 along the Great Northern route to the north.

At the same time, the State Highway Department embarked on a road-building campaign that was to last another 40 years. Farm-to-market roads were built and then surfaced to accommodate increasingly mobile farm and small town residents, who took to the automobile as if they had been born behind the wheel.

Good roads and transportation that needed no oats and hay revolutionized life in rural North Dakota. For the first time, farmers were no longer exclusively linked to the nearest elevator and railroad branch line as a market for their crops. Nor were rural shoppers effectively the captives of the nearest small-town mercantiles. Automobile transportation was their ticket to independence in pleasurable as well as practical pursuits.

North Dakotans delighted in their exciting new range of choices. Their gain, though, guaranteed fewer options to businesses in the smaller markets who could not compete with the variety of merchandise, services and amenities that made large towns into regional magnets.

North Dakota's social conscience was reflected in the large number of institutions established in the constitution to serve the disadvantaged, among them the treatment center for the mentally ill now known as Jamestown State Hospital and the School for the Deaf at Devils Lake (top left and above). San Haven, the state sanatorium at Dunseith, cared for victims of tuberculosis until medicine virtually conquered the disease. Subsequently associated with the State School at Grafton as a center for the care of profoundly mentally retarded individuals, this second role is again being phased out as a result of deinstitutionalization.

Educational institutions have been important to both growth and civic identity throughout North Dakota . . . among them, Minot State College (top left) and Valley City State College (left), both former normal schools which evolved into teachers' colleges and now prepare students for a broad range of professions. Their graduates once made up faculties of small-town schools like that of Alkabo (above); their consolidations and closures encapsulate one reason for broadening of college curricula to present other options. Jamestown College's dramatic Raugust Library (top right) symbolizes the vigor with which the private Presbyterian school has faced persistent challenges.

The heart of the prairie is an exporter of raw materials — durum wheat and barley, beef and sunflowers. But its finest crop of all is talented, ambitious and highly motivated men and women raised in its towns and farmlands who sought achievements on the national scene.

While their cities have grown, the central and northern counties have generally been losing population since the end of World War I. Perhaps that's part of the reason that the region is disproportionately represented on any list of North Dakotans with notable accomplishments...a combination of the disciplined and determined family spirit that has clung to the land, and the limited career opportunities available at home.

These famous expatriates have made their marks in fields as disparate as entertainment and military science, literature and education. Most famous of all are Peggy Lee, who grew up in Wimbledon and Jamestown but went on to be widely regarded as the finest jazz singer of the big band era; and Strasburg's genial accordion maestro, the ageless Lawrence Welk.

Actresses Angie Dickinson of Kulm and Phyllis Frelich of Devils Lake, broadcaster Eric Sevareid of Velva and Louis L'Amour — the Jamestown native who is the most widely published author of all time — all started in the region but found success on other stages. Playwright Maxwell Anderson was from Jamestown. So is Lois Phillips Hudson, whose novel *The Bones of Plenty* has been called the finest fiction written about the Great Depression. Ebony Magazine editor Era Bell Thompson spent her youth on a hard-bitten farm near Steele.

General David Jones, a Minot native, has headed the Joint Chiefs of Staff, and astronaut James Buchli of Jamestown is playing a role in the nation's conquest of space. And the list goes on and on...in scholarship, in business, in exploration.

The heart of the prairie could never entirely satisfy the dreams its founders invested in it. It could never replicate the close and tidy farmlands of the Midwest, the deep civic confidence of long-lived Yankee communities or the urban complexity of the Twin Cities.

But it has proved itself as fertile ground for tough-minded, homegrown cities of a certain realistic size. It has watched them labor to become centers for commerce and culture in the areas they serve, and develop a certain knack for raising another kind of dreams...by nurturing sons and daughters with the right attributes and abilities to set reachable goals, and grasp them.

Natives of the heart of the prairie have made their marks in diverse fields. A sampling: newsman Eric Sevareid of Velva (opposite); prolific author Louis L'Amour of Jamestown; and, clockwise, Broadway actress Phyllis Frelich of Devils Lake, Ebony Magazine editor Era Bell Thompson (shown among her fellow pupils in Steele), champagne music-maker Lawrence Welk of Strasburg, and General David C. Jones of Minot, chairman of the U.S. Joint Chiefs of Staff.

Minot Air Force Base has had dynamic influence on life in Minot, both economically and socially. Thousands of men and women stationed there boast that "only the best come north." Other military installations, however, had little long-term impact, like the short-lived Air Force radar station built at Fortuna.

North Dakota loves its basketball. The high suspense and drama of the annual Class B tournament, pitting partisans of small-town powerhouse teams, has a secondary benefit as well — its enormous economic impact on host communities like Minot.

89

Minot was born as a rowdy encampment of 8,000 railroad workers employed to carry out Jim Hill's ambitious dreams. Today civic amenities include the pleasant lawns and gardens of Roosevelt Park and the wild denizens of nearby Minot Zoo.

Minot's 1986 centennial recaptured a bit of the flavor and costumery of its early days. It showed off the cultural accoutrements of a modern North Dakota community as well in concerts by its centennial band and chorale.

Rural North Dakota congregates in the dense July heat for the annual State Fair at Minot. More than a hundred thousand strong, they find attractions both traditional and contemporary — from its livestock shows and competitions for everything from flower-raising to photography, to the giant midway lighting up the dusk.

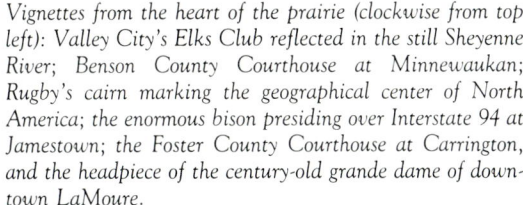

Vignettes from the heart of the prairie (clockwise from top left): Valley City's Elks Club reflected in the still Sheyenne River; Benson County Courthouse at Minnewaukan; Rugby's cairn marking the geographical center of North America; the enormous bison presiding over Interstate 94 at Jamestown; the Foster County Courthouse at Carrington, and the headpiece of the century-old grande dame of downtown LaMoure.

Sod broken by pioneer farmers is still tilled, though elderly homesteads stand lonely on the horizon. They were emptied by the trend to larger, more economical units.

Dryland Farms and Homegrown Industry

*Like liquid gold the wheat field lies
A marvel of yellow and russet and green
That ripples and runs, that floats and flies,
With the subtle shadows...*

*I hear the jocund calls of men
Who sweep amid the ripened grain
With swift, stern reapers; once again
The evening splendor floods the plain:
The crickets' chime
Makes pauseless rhyme,
And toward the sun
The spendid colors romp and run
Before the wind's feet
In the wheat!*

(From "Dakota Wheat Field" by Hamlin Garland)

Wheat is the prairie's marvel. It has been, since plow sliced sod, and forever will be as long as bread is baked to feed a hungry world.

But the devotion to wheat dating back to homestead days has also been part of the region's burden. Pioneer farmers regarded wheat as the king of crops. A lot was good; more would be even better.

Tens of thousands of plows turned sod from the South Dakota border to the Canadian line beginning in the 1880s and continuing with renewed vigor during the second great settlement boom from 1898 until World War I.

Some of the freshly broken fields were flat, well-drained and fertile. Some were sparse and rocky. Perhaps half of the new Dakota farming class understood the rudiments of agriculture. The rest were drawn by ambitious plans to make fortunes as land prices increased, counting on periodic upturns in the grain markets as indicators of the prosperity they had in store for them.

It was a great experiment, and not all the results yielded good news. Farming methods brought from damper regions turned the topsoil to fine dust, and the endless winds blew it out toward Missouri. Single-minded devotion to growing wheat mined the soil, and yields dropped. Disease ravaged early, non-resistant varieties. Markets wobbled; good crops never insured a profit.

But experience and research, much of it conducted by the North Dakota Agricultural Experiment Stations, combined to improve wheat farmers' odds at the same time that the gospel of diversification began to be preached in earnest. Combined with a strong conservation movement dating from the Dirty '30s, the knowledge gained over the years has helped adjust the region's agricultural economy to suit the land's advantages and minimize its shortcomings.

The dust storms of the Dirty '30s brought new vigor to the campaign to preserve the state's most valuable resource by preventing soil erosion. In this 1939 photo, high school girls hoe a windbreak near Carrington.

Like farms across the state, those at the heart of the prairie still rate wheat Number One...not only modern varieties of spring wheat, in which the state leads the nation, but also durum wheat. North Dakota produces the lion's share of the nation's durum, a crop introduced from Russia during the influx of German-Russian immigrants during the 1890s.

The two wheats compliment each other in the kitchen. Spring wheat is known for its high protein content, the quality that inspired Minneapolis millers at the start of the era of bonanza farms. Durum, on the other hand, is ideal to process into semolina, the grainy golden powder used in making pasta.

Other grain crops have proven themselves as well — or better — suited to growing conditions of central and northern North Dakota. The state leads the nation in production of barley as well as the two wheats. Its requirements for a shorter growing season and less intense heat to ripen have made it ideal as a northern crop.

While the three crops are scattered across the state's midsection, different areas top the list as top producers. Durum is concentrated in the so-called Durum Triangle, the counties of Williams, Bottineau, Ward, Mountrail, Towner, Ramsey and Benson. Spring wheat yields west of the Red River Valley rank highest in Barnes, Stutsman and McLean Counties, while the largest producers of barley — again, outside the Valley — are Cavalier, Towner and Ramsey.

Rye, once considered a weed infesting wheat fields, has become a fourth grain in which the state tops U.S. producers. Highest production is in Ransom, Sargent, Richland, LaMoure, Dickey and Stutsman Counties. The band of central counties between Canada and South Dakota also harvests more flax than any other state.

The story of sunflowers illustrates the pluses and pitfalls of diversification. The tall, stately wildflower was a part of the North American landscape long before the first white men set foot on the continent. It became a minor specialty crop nearly a century ago, sold roasted and salted as the snack known as "Russian peanuts."

In the 1970s improved varieties and cultivation techniques brought it to the fields of North Dakota, which continues to raise nearly all of America's harvest of both the confection and oil varieties. Processing plants were built in several cities including Velva, based on high hopes for the polyunsaturated oil yielded by the seeds and high-protein by-products like livestock feeds.

But ups and downs in world markets have shadowed original optimistic projections. Patience as well as agricultural savvy is apparently required before the new crop brings about the major economic impact its backers have expected.

While grains and specialty crops — including smatterings of buckwheat, mustard, potatoes, soybeans and others — remain the mainstays of agricultural income, livestock is a part of the heritage as well as current operations of central Dakota farmers.

The original settlers in portions of the midsection, especially in the Souris River loop, were ranchers. Beef cattle continue to be an important part of many central North Dakota agricultural operations in combination with grain and forage crops. Lands never suited to the plow have gradually been returned to grazing in these areas.

The state's first land-hungry farmers found all too soon that the earth they claimed was only one part of the three-sided farming equation.

While they concentrated first on digging and improving it, they turned attention too toward the other elements farther beyond their control — water and the markets.

The vagaries of the wheat market were the center of debate and angry discontent almost from the time that railroad lines threw up elevators to collect the harvest. Decades of dissatisfaction with the price manipulations of rail barons and Minneapolis millers inspired widespread support of the Farmers Union and then formation of the Nonpartisan League.

Both movements for better prices found their greatest support in the heart of the prairie, where the Farmers Union continues to work actively. They advocated the principle of farmer control. Contemporary reminders of their successes range from cooperative elevators and stores, to the nation's only state-owned mill and elevator.

For a time North Dakota earned the reputation of the most radical state in the nation for its farmers' support of these socialistic projects. The wild politics of the years during and after World War I have faded into history along with the names of central characters like A.C. Townley, Lynn Frazier and William Langer and the League's main opponent, the Independent Voters Association.

Farmers and their political spokesmen have attempted to confront the vicissitudes of the weather as well as those of outside markets, and with equally mixed results.

The Garrison Diversion Project was conceived to bypass North Dakota's scanty and sporadic rainfall by bringing a man-made river east and south across the heart of the prairie. Envisioned as North Dakota's salvation during the driest years of the Great Depression, it was to be the federal government's payoff for the rich bottomlands inundated by the reservoir of Garrison Dam.

The original ambitious proposal drew bold lines across a map of the midsection of

U.S. Senator Quentin Burdick and Representatives Mark Andrews and Tom Kleppe attended the ground-breaking for the McClusky Canal in May of 1970. Still far from completion or resolution, Garrison Diversion was envisioned nearly 50 years ago as an antidote to the periodic droughts that ravage central North Dakota.

the state, with deep broad excavated channels flowing toward Devils Lake, then down to the Oakes area. Farmers would draw on the waters for irrigation, introducing humid crops to semi-arid country. Recreation would boom in the project's wake — boating, fishing, beach parties in the midst of prairie grasses.

It was to be one of the greatest engineering marvels in the history of mankind, and it was mired in controversy almost from the moment draglines began biting huge mouthsful of soil to carve the first miles of canal.

Today the embattles project continues to move forward slowly toward a far more modest goal, steadily whittled down by opposition from landowners in its path, wildlife advocates and the government of Manitoba. Instead of the water for which farmers yearned, it has drawn the storm clouds.

The most gargantuan engineering project in the history of North Dakota has brought the man-made river of the McClusky Canal snaking across the center of the state. Congressional appropriations have greatly slowed progress on construction, with the state's Washington delegation negotiating with opposition ranging from the Canadian government to wildlife advocates.

Through Garrison Diversion, Missouri River waters have begun to irrigate farm acreage in some areas ranging from Velva to Oakes. A scaled-down project continues to fight for its survival.

The prairie's bounty includes more than wheat. The Ladish Malting Plant at Spiritwood processes home-grown barley. The same is true of sunflowers, well suited to climate and culture but battered by an erratic market . . . as well as by clouds of well-fed blackbirds (above). Farmers resort to a variety of measures including shotguns to shoo them away; since the birds are protected, the shots are intended to scare rather than slaughter.

Ranching preceded farming in parts of central and northern North Dakota, especially along the Souris River from Towner to Kenmare and in the south central counties. Hay — a major crop in the region — is better known for its end-product, prime beefsteak.

Human agriculture has finally learned from the prairie's past and returned it to the crop for which much of it is best suited — lush grasses. Cattle and horses dine on luxuriant spring growth. Regional breeders race thoroughbreds and other breeds at events like the Wells County Fair and on the professional circuit.

North Dakota farmers like Ardon Herman have put their ingenuity to work at inventing equipment like the Herman Diamond Disc that's better-suited to the demands of Dakota Land.

Agriculture divides the year into two main seasons — spring field work and summer harvests.

Most crops of the prairie are stored for shipment to market as a raw product. But young homegrown industries like Noodles by Leonardo at Cando have set out to process certain products — here, durum wheat — for shipment to market in finished form. Spaghetti, macaroni and other pastas depend on locally-milled semolina for their distinctive taste, color and texture.

Diversification is an economic principle taken to heart not only by agriculture but by local and state promoters of industrial development. Success stories include the progress of Western Gear, a defense contractor which manufactures sophisticated weapons devices at its Jamestown plant. The oil industry has run through its boom-and-bust cycle several times since discovery of oil at Tioga 35 years ago; these workers are stationed near Westhope.

Left behind by the glaciers and gathered by man, rocks still punctuate some wide-open North Dakota vistas — though many were buried during the prosperous 1970s by farmers tired of tilling around them. Potholes present another obstacle to the farmer's dream of the endless arrow-straight furrow.

Punctuating Nature

When America remembers the heart of the prairie, it thinks not of what is there to be seen, but what is not.

It is a land that perplexes the postcard-makers. Its surprises are horizontal, not vertical. Even its Turtle Mountains are really a medium-sized ridge. Its thousand treeless lakes and ponds are merely blue freckles on the broad flat green face of the plains.

To the native or the adopted fan, though, nowhere does the landscape offer quite the same freedom and sense of possibilities.

That sense can be deceptive, as history demonstrates. Yet there is no landscape that so strongly relates, not to the earth, but to the sky; not to the geographic remnants of eons past memory, but to a country still in the making.

In a crowded world, this emptiness can take your breath away. Pause at the top of a stone-strewn hill in the south central counties, and stand at the center of 360 degrees of silence. Chances are that no clamouring human enterprise intrudes in a vista that stretches dozens of miles.

Drive the northern route in late September during the small hours of the morning — the hours when even the bravest pull the shades and stoke the fire against the prairie's solemn vastness. The land seems to fall away, an ocean of blackness cut by the twin beams of your headlights and if you're very lucky, the receding red taillights of fellow travelers. The Aurora Borealis dance overhead in the crisp autumn air, giggling beams and Milky Ways of light that tease of a glowing city — or a universe — just beyond the horizon.

Watch the sun rise much too late for breakfast on a January morning. Its pink and orange light curdles into high winter wisps of cloud before the sky turns bluer than blue, farther than far away, and the brief day begins.

It is a land cut out for powerful strides, a land designed for epics. Evidence of battles lost can persevere for 50 years in tinder-dry farm buildings staring blankly across still-tilled fields. Victory remains a harvest triumphant over drought, or grasshoppers, or the plague of a market glutted with others' bounty.

The prairie remains a wild land, but it has been tested. Courage has faced its daunting breed of grandeur, and has tried, and sometimes it has won.

The pride is not only in the victories, but in taking up the challenge.

Upon the plains a man is tall;
no so, a man beside the sea.
Dwarfed by the gray cliff's granite face
and by the breaker's foamy length,
a man is small;
a tiny looker-on is he,
defied by an immensity
beyond control.
But on the plains a man can stride
with giant strength.
His stubborn fields are bleak and wide
and roofed with space,
yet there he knows his mastery.
Upon the plains no breakers roll,
no purple mountain-shadows fall,
and man is tall.

—"Stature" by Prudence Gearey Sand

Nature sports its special spectrum in Turtle Mountain birch trees against a cobalt sky, in the green of young crops against black earth, in blue waves of blooming flax, and in the harmony of verdant fields, creekside cottonwoods and clouds.

North Dakotans have always equated water not only with crops, but with relaxation. The steamer Minnie H traversed Devils Lake from cityside to the chautauqua grounds at Lakewood Park, where crowds of thousands awaited nationally-known speakers and entertainers. The dance pavilion on the shore of Spiritwood Lake drew thousands of romantics, too, with evenings of music sometimes featuring noted bands of the day. Excursion boats cruised the Sheyenne River, too, on pleasant day outings from Valley City.

Little-known monuments preserve mysteries and journeys of days beyond memory. At Alkabo, a historic site displays Writing Rock, its hieroglyphics presumably carved by ancient Indians or their ancestors. The spherical David Thompson Memorial near Verendrye commemorates the British geographer who explored the center of the continent on the eve of the 19th century. A modern Highway Department marker recounts the legend of Crystal Springs.

The region offers a variety of sites, sports and attractions, from the authentic Danish mill at Kenmare and golf courses like the stream-crossing links at Crosby to Fort Ransom's Sheyenne River Arts and Crafts Festival and cross-country skiing along a frozen creek.

Prairie lakes offer a few resorts, like Red Willow near Binford (top right), and a lot of wide-open water for fishing. While walleyes are the fish of choice, toothy northern pike offer exciting sport.

The International Peace Garden marks the midpoint of the longest peaceful border in the world with natural forests, jewel-like lakes and a bevy of floral gardens adding color to its Turtle Mountain setting. Development continues; not shown in the aerial view is the stately Peace Tower.

Young people from throughout the United States and Canada come to the Peace Garden each summer to attend the International Music Camp. Musical excellence is its primary objective, though other sessions range from drama to dance.

Lake Metigoshe is a summer address of hundreds of North Dakotans and a favorite temporary destination of thousands more who enjoy boating or camping at Lake Metigoshe State Park.

Fall accents the woods meandering along the course of the Sheyenne River.

Crisp fall days present the Turtle Mountains in their finest form.

Skiers enjoy one of North Dakota's rarest commodities along with one more familiar — steep hills and snow — at Bottineau Winter Park.

Steep slopes are not a prerequisite for winter recreation. Cross-country skiing is popular in the Turtle Mountains (along with many other areas), along with snowmobiling along trails among the leafless skeletons of bare trees.

The earth is its heart, but water is the lifeblood of the prairie — channeled broad and straight by man, or slowly coursing in crooked giggling streams etched by nature.

Humans have dug deep into the prairie but lightly skim the surface of its lakes. Brightly-colored catamarans race on Devils Lake's Creel Bay in the annual Creel Cup Regatta.

Nancy Edmonds Hanson is a frequent contributor to *North Dakota Horizons* and other regional and national magazines, and is director of public relations with Hetland Ltd. of Fargo. Raised in Hillsboro and Streeter, she has written a national bestselling guide for freelance writers; produced a weekly news program for statewide public television; edited a variety of periodicals, and founded Prairie House, a publisher of regional books. The former Fargo *Forum* reporter and assistant state travel director attended Concordia College and graduated from Moorhead State University in 1971.

Sheldon Green is the editor of *North Dakota Horizons* Magazine. A native of Hatton, he graduated from the University of North Dakota in 1971. He was editor of the Hazen Star for ten years during the time of coal conversion development in western North Dakota. Green has also worked for daily newspapers in Idaho and Green Bay, Wisconsin, where he developed and edited a weekend magazine supplement. His writing, photography and design have won several awards and his work has appeared in national publications. He lives with his wife and family in Bismarck.

Russ Hanson is director of photography with Hetland Ltd. of Fargo. Formerly chairman of Bismarck Junior College's graphic arts department, the Mandan native has contributed photographs to a long list of state, regional and national books and periodicals, from *North Dakota Horizons* to *Midwest Living* to National Geographic Books. He is a 1968 graduate of BJC and earned his degree in photography and cinematography from Southern Illinois University in 1970. He, his wife Nancy and their daughter Patti live in Fargo-Moorhead.

Acknowledgements:
  The board of directors and staff of the Greater North Dakota Association, without whose approval and support this project would not be possible.
  Additional photographs by Nancy Edmonds Hanson; Mark Nelson, Minot; Larry Simpson, Fargo; Peter Herman, Brinsmade; Gary Redmann, Bismarck; and *North Dakota Horizons* Magazine.

State Historical Society photo archivist Todd Strand.
The Institute of Regional Studies, for the use of its fine library.
Steve Gorman, for his encouragement.

Bibliography

American Guide Series. *North Dakota, A Guide to the Northern Prairie State*. New York: Oxford University Press, 1938; second edition, 1950.

Eidem, R.J., and Goodman, L.R. *The Atlas of North Dakota*. Fargo ND: North Dakota Studies Inc., 1976.

Hudson, John C. *Plains Country Towns*. Minneapolis MN: University of Minnesota Press, 1985.

Jelliff, Theodore B. *North Dakota, A Living Legacy*. Fargo ND: K&K Publishers, 1983.

Johnsgard, Paul A., *Birds of the Great Plains*. Lincoln NE: University of Nebraska Press, 1979.

Lamar, Howard Roberts, *Dakota Territory 1861-1889*. New Haven CT: Yale University Press, 1956.

Leifur, Conrad W. *Our State North Dakota*. New York: American Book Company, 1942; revised 1945 and 1953.

Palmer, Bertha Rachael, *Beauty Spots of North Dakota*. Boston MA: The Gorham Press, 1928.

Remington, Frederic, *Stubble and Slough in Dakota*. Fargo ND: The Box Elder Bug Press, 1975. (Reprinted from Harper's Monthly, May 1892.)

Robinson, Elwyn B. *History of North Dakota*. Lincoln NE: University of Nebraska Press, 1966.

Sandoz, Mari, *The Buffalo Hunters*. Lincoln NE: University of Nebraska Press, 1954 and 1978.

Sevareid, Eric, *Not So Wild a Dream*. New York: Alfred A. Knopf, Inc., 1946.

Sherman, William C. *Prairie Mosaic, An Ethnic Atlas of Rural North Dakota*. Fargo ND: Institute for Regional Studies, 1983.

Smorada, James, and Lois Forrest, editors, *Century of Stories — Jamestown and Stutsman County*. Jamestown ND: Fort Seward Historical Society, Inc., 1983.

Wemett, William Marks, *The Story of the Flickertail State*. Valley City ND: By the author, 1923.

Williams, Mary Ann Barnes, *Origins of North Dakota Place Names*. Bismarck ND: By the author, 1966; reprinted by McLean County Historical Society, 1973.

NORTH DAKOTA BANKERS ASSOCIATION

Harvey H. Huber, President
John W. Pierson, President-Elect
Roger Berglund, Vice President/Treasurer

The Dakota Graphic Society gratefully acknowledges these sponsors of Volume Three of The North Dakota Centennial Series...

NORTHWEST

Bottineau
  First National Bank
  State Bank of Bottineau
Westhope
  Peoples State Bank
Bowbells
  First National Bank
Powers Lake
  Liberty State Bank
Crosby
  Farmers State Bank
  First National Bank
Drake
  First National Bank
Towner
  State Bank of Towner
Velva
  Peoples State Bank
Watford City
  First International Bank
  McKenzie County National Bank
Garrison
  Garrison State Bank
New Town
  Lakeside State Bank
Parshall
  Peoples State Bank
Stanley
  Scandia American Bank
Rugby
  First American Bank
  Merchants Bank
Mohall
  Citizens State Bank
Dunseith
  Security State Bank
Rolette
  Rolette State Bank
Rolla
  First Bank of Rolla
Minot
  First American Bank & Trust
  First Bank of North Dakota-Minot
  First Western Bank
  Norwest Bank Minot
Harvey
  First State Bank
  The National Bank of Harvey
Ray
  Citizens State Bank
Tioga
  The Bank of Tioga
Williston
  American State Bank & Trust Company
  First National Bank & Trust Company
  Williston Basin State Bank

NORTHEAST

Leeds
  Farmers State Bank
Maddock
  Farmers State Bank
Minnewaukan
  First American Bank
Langdon
  Farmers & Merchants Bank
  First Bank of Langdon
Munich
  First State Bank
Grand Forks
  Community National Bank
  The Dakota Bank
  First Bank of North Dakota-Grand Forks
  First National Bank in Grand Forks
  Valley Bank and Trust Company
Larimore
  First American Bank
Northwood
  Northwood State Bank
McVille
  McVille State Bank
Michigan
  Lamb's Bank of Michigan City
Petersburg
  Citizens State Bank
Tolna
  Farmers & Merchants State Bank
Cavalier
  Citizens State Bank
  First State Bank
Drayton
  Drayton State Bank
Hamilton
  Bank of Hamilton
Walhalla
  Walhalla State Bank
Devils Lake
  First National Bank
  Ramsey National Bank & Trust Co.
  Western State Bank
Cando
  First State Bank
  Towner County State Bank
Buxton
  First State Bank
Hatton
  Farmers & Merchants National Bank
Hillsboro
  Norwest Bank Hillsboro
Mayville
  The Goose River Bank
Portland
  First & Farmers Bank
Adams
  Security State Bank
Grafton
  First American Bank & Trust Company
  Norwest Bank Grafton, N.A.
Lankin
  Citizens State Bank
Minto
  Bank of Minto
Park River
  First State Bank

SOUTHEAST

Fingal
  Fingal State Bank
Litchville
  Litchville State Bank
Valley City
  Farmers & Merchants State Bank
  First National Bank
  Norwest Bank Valley City
Wimbledon
  Farmers & Merchants Bank
Arthur
  First State Bank
Buffalo
  First State Bank
Casselton
  First American Bank
  First State Bank
Fargo
  Dakota Bank & Trust Company
  Fargo National Bank & Trust Company
  First Bank of North Dakota-Fargo
  Norwest Bank Fargo
  State Bank of Fargo
  Union State Bank
Harwood
  Harwood State Bank
Hunter
  Security State Bank
Kindred
  Kindred State Bank
Page
  Page State Bank
West Fargo
  First State Bank of West Fargo
  West Fargo State Bank
Ellendale
  First National Bank & Trust Company
Oakes
  First National Bank of Oakes
New Rockford
  First State Bank
Sheyenne
  Farmers & Merchants Bank
Carrington
  Farmers State Bank
  First American Bank & Trust Company
Cooperstown
  Farmers & Merchants Bank
  First State Bank
Hannaford
  Security State Bank
Robinson
  Security State Bank
Steele
  Bank of Steele
Edgeley
  Security National Bank
Kulm
  Kulm State Bank
LaMoure
  First State Bank
Marion
  State Bank of Marion
Gackle
  First State Bank
Napoleon
  Stock Growers Bank
Ashley
  McIntosh County Bank
Lehr
  Central Dakota Bank
Wishek
  Security State Bank
Enderlin
  Citizens State Bank
  Peoples & Enderlin State Bank
Lisbon
  First American Bank
Fairmore
  Peoples State Bank
Hankinson
  Lincoln State Bank
Lidgerwood
  First National Bank
Wahpeton
  Dakota Bank & Trust Company
  First Bank of North Dakota-Wahpeton
  Norwest Bank Wahpeton
Forman
  Sargent County Bank
Milnor
  First National Bank
Finley
  Citizens State Bank
Hope
  First State Bank
Sharon
  First State Bank
Jamestown
  First Bank of North Dakota-Jamestown
  Norwest Bank Jamestown
Streeter
  State Bank of Streeter
Ypsilanti
  Farmers State Bank
Fessenden
  First National Bank

SOUTHWEST

Hettinger
  First National Bank
  West River State Bank
Bowman
  Dakota Western Bank
  First National Bank
Bismarck
  Bank of North Dakota
  Bismarck State Bank
  Dakota Bank & Trust Company
  First National Bank & Trust Company
  Norwest Bank Bismarck
  United Bank of Bismarck
Halliday
  The Union Bank
Killdeer
  American State Bank
Hazelton
  Bank of Hazelton
Linton
  First National Bank
Strasburg
  Strasburg State Bank
Carson
  First Southwest Bank
Elgin
  Farmers State Bank
New Leipzig
  First State Bank
Mott
  Commercial Bank of Mott
New England
  American State Bank
Regent
  First State Bank
Turtle Lake
  Bank of Turtle Lake
Underwood
  First Security Bank
Washburn
  Farmers Security Bank
Wilton
  First State Bank
Beulah
  Bank of Beulah
  Security State Bank
Hazen
  Union State Bank
Glen Ullin
  Bank of Glen Ullin
Hebron
  Security Bank of Hebron
Mandan
  First Southwest Bank
  Norwest Bank Mandan
New Salem
  Security State Bank
Center
  State Bank of Oliver County
Goodrich
  First State Bank
McClusky
  First National Bank
Belfield
  First National Bank
Dickinson
  American State Bank & Trust Company
  First National Bank & Trust Company
  Liberty National Bank & Trust Company
Richardton
  First American Bank